Kevin was happily playing today.

Then, he stepped on something and fell down.

"Ouch!"

Kevin rubbed his sore knee and checked what he stepped on.

It was his favorite robot toy.

"Are you okay, Kevin?"

"Yes, I'm okay."

Mom helped Kevin stand up.

"You need to put away toys you're not playing with. Otherwise, you might get hurt like now."

"But I was going to play with it again later."

"That's why you need to put it away. If you leave it out, you might forget where you left it."

Mom was right. Kevin often lost his toys.

"And if someone accidentally kicks it, it could break. Then you can't play with it anymore."

"Okay, Mom. I'll put my toys away."

Kevin put his toys in the toy box. This way, he could find them easily when he wanted to play again.

Put away toys after playing. This way, you won't lose them and can play with them for a long time.

The next day, Kevin came back after playing outside with his friends.

Mom stopped Kevin from going straight to his room.

"Kevin, you need to wash your hands after playing outside."

"But I didn't play with dirt today."

"You still need to wash your hands. If you don't, you could get sick."

When you play outside, you can get invisible germs on your hands. Even if you can't see them, these germs can make you sick if you don't wash them off.

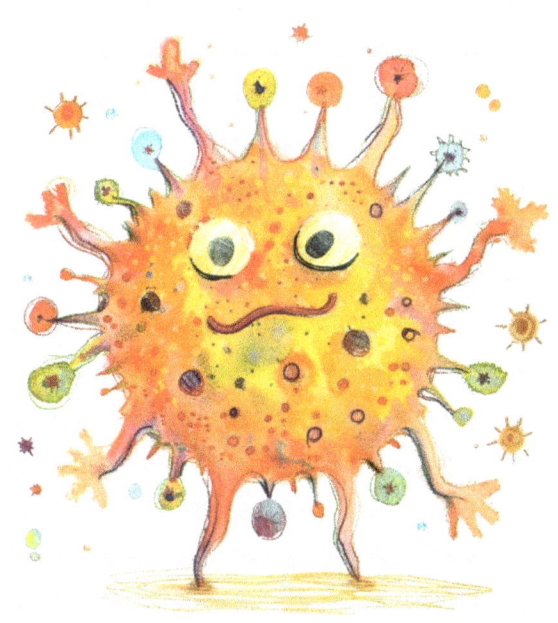

"And if you touch things around the house with dirty hands, you can make Mom and Dad sick too."

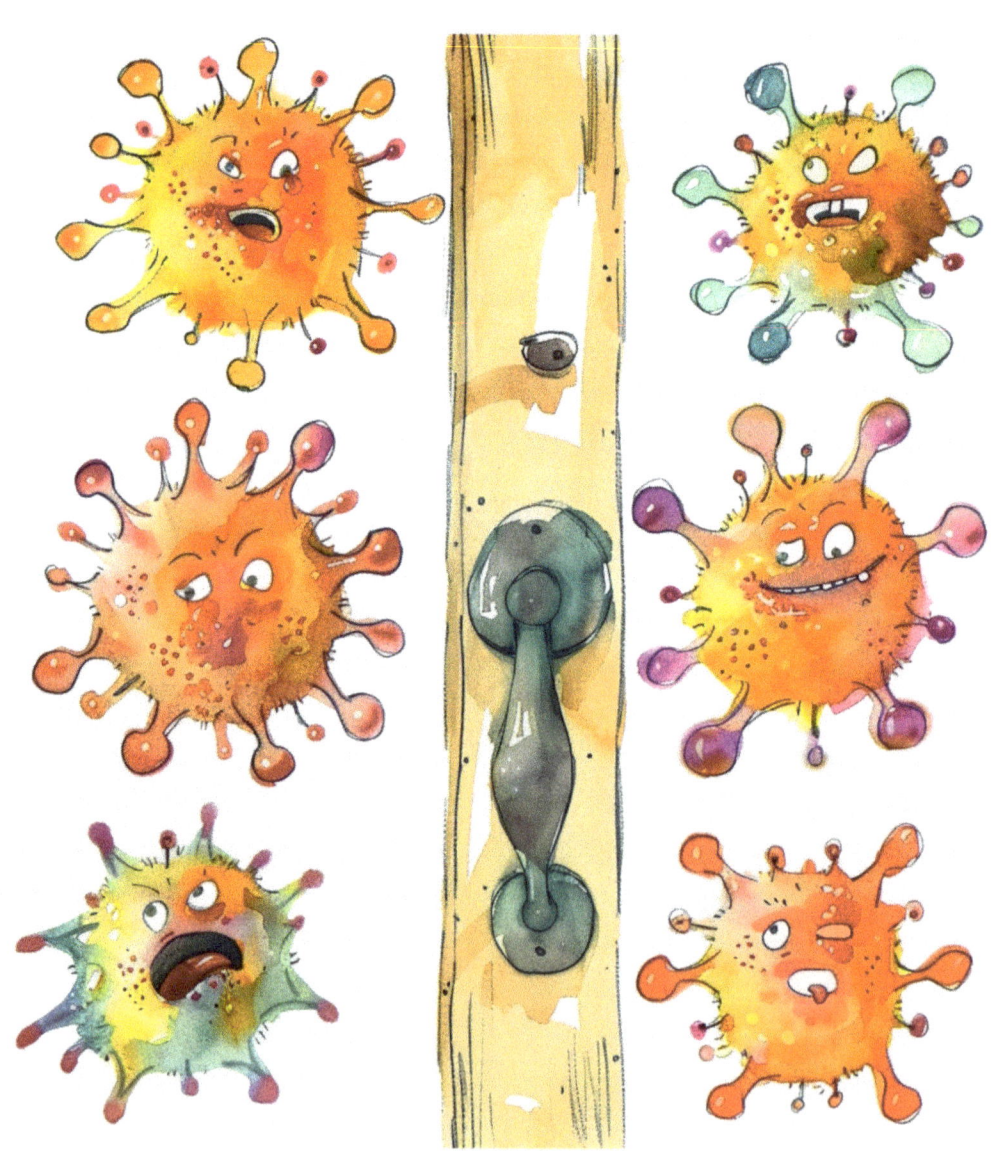

"Okay, I'll wash my hands."

Kevin hurried to the sink. He used soap to wash his palms, the backs of his hands, between his fingers, and under his nails. Mom patted Kevin's head proudly.

Wash your hands after playing outside. Wash your palms, the backs of your hands, between your fingers, and under your nails.

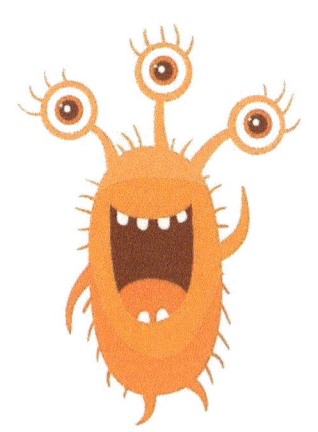 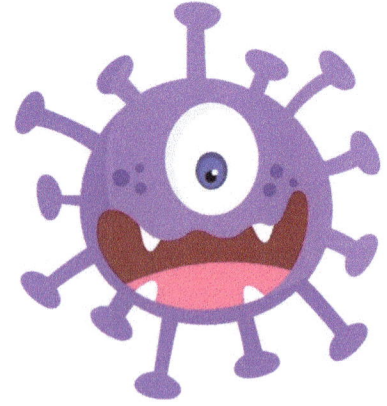

That evening, Dad brought home a cake that Kevin loved. Kevin was excited and ate the cake.

After Kevin finished, Mom said,

"Kevin, you need to brush your teeth after eating cake."

"Why?"

"Sweet foods stick to your teeth and make germs grow. This can cause cavities."

Cavities hurt and make your breath smell bad. If you don't brush your teeth, they can become weak. When your teeth are weak, you can't eat delicious foods.

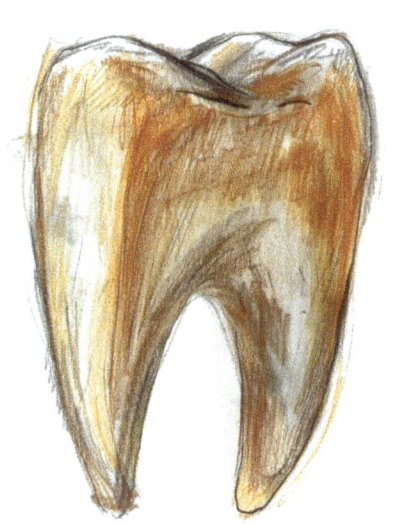

"Or do you want to go to the dentist again like last time?"

"No! I'll brush my teeth."

Kevin remembered the last time he had to get a tooth pulled at the dentist. He quickly went to the sink and brushed his teeth for 3 minutes, just like the dentist showed him. He brushed the front, back, and chewing surfaces of his teeth.

"How do they look?"

Kevin proudly showed his clean teeth to Mom and Dad. They hugged Kevin tightly.

Brush your teeth after eating. Brush for 3 minutes, covering all parts of your mouth.

Honglee books recommended books

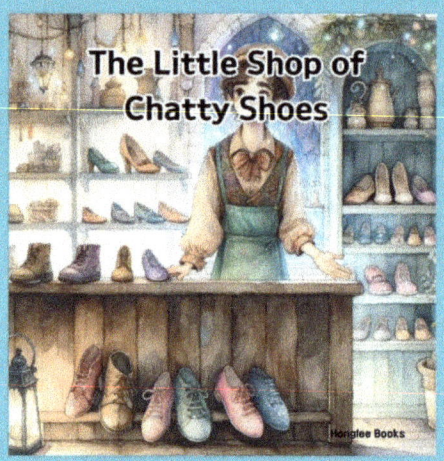

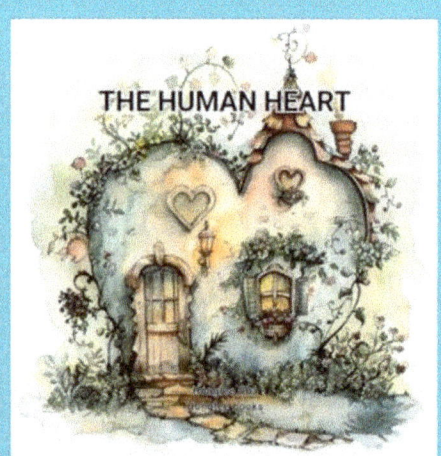

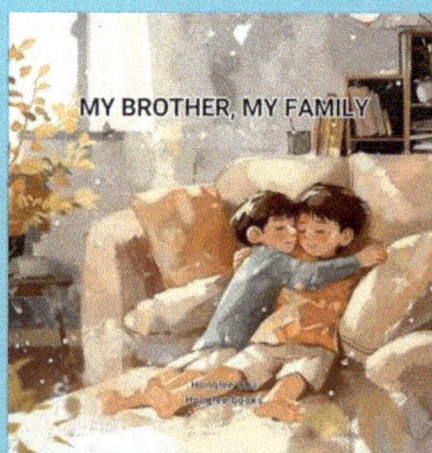

Honglee books recommended Educational Books

The Olympics Swimming Manual

The Soccer Manual

The Break dance Manual

The Gymnastics Manual

The Track and Field Manual

Honglee books recommended series

John mystery story

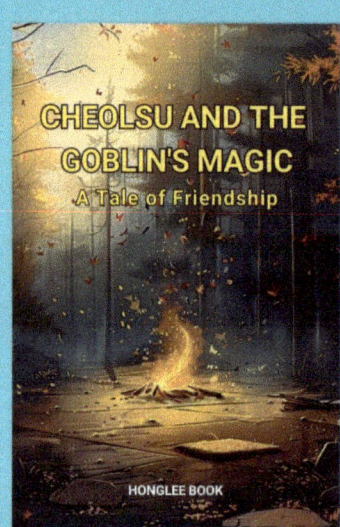
Choelsu special story

Kid Detectives story

Hello! Hongleebooks is a place where the seeds of imagination are planted, and the flowers of dreams bloom. Turning our pages is not just reading; it's an invitation for children to dive into the infinite world of imagination. By providing books filled with magical stories and vivid characters, we enable children to discover their true selves and experience the world from various perspectives.

At Hongleebooks, we believe every book is a world, and every page unfolds a journey of new possibilities. With us, children will spread the wings of their imagination, dream their own dreams, and learn valuable life lessons. We support them in envisioning and creating a brighter future.

Together, we are building a world where imagination becomes reality. Hongleebooks is a place for children to dream, learn, and imagine. Join us in our story.

www.ingramcontent.com/pod-product-compliance
Lightning Source LLC
LaVergne TN
LVHW070540070526
838199LV00076B/6818